BEFORE THE RAIN BEGAN

BEFORE THE RAIN BEGAN

and other poems

DELL ALLEN

TORTOISE PRESS

© Tortoise Press 1975
Recess
County Galway
Ireland

ISBN 0 905030 00 1

Set in Monotype Bembo
Made and printed in the Republic of Ireland by Mount Salus Press,
Tritonville Road, Dublin 4.

CONTENTS

For Kevin Joyce

Before the Rain Began

I met two Kerry women between Dingle and Slea Head,
They wore black Kerry cloaks, hoods lined with cherry red.
They told me I should hurry, that rain was on the way,
Across the Blasket Islands lay a dusky patch of grey.
In softly-spoken gaelic they blessed the travelling man,
But I was back in Annascaul before the rain began.

I met two Kerry girls between Dublin and Glencree,
Clad in slacks and sweaters, free as the wind is free.
They told me I should hurry, that rain was overhead,
Dark clouds were slowly merging beyond the Feather Bed.
In softly-spoken gaelic they blessed the travelling man,
But I was home in Stepaside before the rain began.

Connemara

Turf-cutters by the Clifden road,
A flock of sheep beyond Recess,
The gypsies with their pots and pans,
Their ponies, goats and caravans,
Their languid air, their casual dress.
With peaks outlined against the sky,
Like sentinels the mountains stand
Where Tullycross and Renvyle meet
And Kylemore finds a quiet retreat
Beyond Lough Ina's pebbled strand.

The tangled heather blooms beside
Gorse bushes washed by summer rain,
As sunset dyes the waves with red,
Dark curraghs loom around the Head,
Oars creaking as the rowlocks strain.
The road curves inward by the sea,
Zigzagging on capriciously
By fuchsia blooms, by low stone walls,
Threading its way to Aasleagh Falls
Where Errif flows to Killary.

*   *   *

No traffic signals call a halt
Where mountain roadways twist and meet.
No neon lights spell out their signs,
No lighted lamp at dusk outlines
The signposts in a village street . . .
But, through the valleys, dawn or dusk,
Where trout streams murmur ceaselessly
By narrow sheep tracks where I knew
Long years ago bilberries grew—
There would I walk unerringly.

I Built a House

I built a house in Aughrus Beg,
I spread the roof with thatch;
The door which faces to the hill,
Each chimney pot, each sash and sill
Is painted red to match.

I was the builder of my house,
I was the builder's mate;
I was the architect who planned,
Who carried timber, bricks and sand,
Unwearied by their weight.

I built it in a sheltered spot
Above the water's edge,
Where heather quilts a purple bed
And slender woodbine cranes its head
Across the fuchsia hedge.

I've got a black three-legged pot
That squats beside the fire,
A wooden pail, a rocking chair,
A crock or two of earthenware—
What else should I require?

I gather mushrooms in the dawn,
And cockles at ebb-tide.
Have herrings when the crews come in
Or lobsters, if my luck is in,
Cooked by the chimney side.

It's peaceful on an autumn eve
When sunset sweeps the bay,
The windows catch the golden light,
The door stays open day and night
For all who pass that way.

When on the Clifden road at dusk
A fairy candle gleams;
If you can read the fairy sign
Perhaps you'll find that house of mine:
I built it in my dreams.

Coming Home

From gable to gable we'll whitewash the house,
Put a new coat of paint on the door,
We'll pebble the pathway and trim up the hedge,
We'll put boxes of flowers on each window ledge
And buy a new broom for the floor.

We'll whitewash the wall that leads down to the gate
Where the blooms of the fuchsia are red,
Scour the kitchen as clean as a bright new pin,
Put curtains of lace on the windows within,
New thatch on the roof overhead.

We'll bleach the best cloth in the meadow until
It is whiter than fresh fallen snow.
We'll tidy the dresser and scrub every shelf,
We'll brighten it up with a new set of delph
And the old lustre jugs in a row.

We'll cook a plump chicken—she likes a pot roast—
Serve it up on the blue willow plate.
The hearth will be swept and the fire will be bright,
The lamp will be trimmed and just ready to light
At the window, in case she is late.

I know she'll look out for the things of her youth:
For her name that she carved on a tree,
The churning of butter, the fresh oven bread,
Her old patchwork quilt that she liked on her bed
Since she was the height of my knee.

So I'll wait by the fire until she comes in,
'Twill be just like the old days, I know:
She'll steal in on tip-toe to spring a surprise
And stand there a moment—a smile in her eyes—
As often she stood long ago.

From Galway to Soho

As I was scanning the bill of fare
The waiter hovered beside my chair,
"We've Galway salmon", I heard him declare,
And then in a low, confiding tone:
"We've turbot, halibut, sole-on-the-bone,
But our salmon is best and widely known!"

He walked away with his step so light
His folded napkin gleaming white,
I knew of course he was perfectly right,
But what could a London waiter know
In a crowded café in Soho,
Where the shaded lights were dim and low,
Of the Salmon Weir and the Claddagh fleet
In the city where Bay and Corrib meet
In the twisted length of a Galway street?

How would these 'tails' that he wore compare
With an Aran jacket in old Eyre Square
Or a bawneen seen at a Galway Fair?
What could he know of the purple and grey
Of an autumn twilight athwart the Bay,
Or the magic scent of new mown hay?

* * *

Disturbing my dreams, as I sat in state,
He brought me the fish disguised on a plate
Garnished with sauces up-to-date!

In cantankerous manner I began:
"I'd rather it fried on a sizzling pan,
Or grilled in butter—I'm a country man!"
He served me the fish in Soho style,
Fidgeting there by my side awhile,
On his face the ghost of a quizzical smile.

"Sure that's how I'd like it myself tonight—
In a nest of mushrooms, am I right?
In the flickering rays of the candlelight
No booking tables in advance,
No dazzling menus worded in France,
No one to give me a curious glance.
But a cosy corner beside the fire,
With the salmon grilled to your heart's desire,
What more, indeed, would a man require?"

Was he assuming the brogue of the West,
Making of me the butt of his jest?
But I waited until I heard the rest:
"I played as a child by the Corrib Weir
And I watched the salmon many a year
When the day was bright and the water clear;
Saw the Cliffs of Moher in kindly weather,
The Aran Islands huddled together,
Each curragh passing, light as a feather;
Dun Aengus battling through wind and rain
And a blackbird's song in a Galway lane—
Sure I often think of those days in vain!"

He walked away in his black and white,
With a step that seemed no longer light,
And a mist came up and clouded my sight . . .
When I cross the Weir in the sunset's glow,
I think of him shuffling to and fro
In that crowded café in Soho!

The Road to Cleggan

I'll take the road to Cleggan
The road that skirts the hill,
An easy road to follow,
No traffic in the hollow
Another mile to go—but I am dreaming still.

The bay will stretch before me,
Boats clustered round the pier,
With groups of men preparing
For fishing and seafaring
To carry on the old tradition year by year.

Then through the fishing village
To the inn beside the pier,
Visitors with city news,
Artists there exchanging views with
Fishermen and farmers from places far and near.

Some folk here I used to know,
But the years are changing fast;
Should I choose to wander
Among the foothills yonder,
Perhaps someone might join me, someone from the past.

I'll take the road to Cleggan
The road that skirts the hill,
An easy road to follow,
No traffic in the hollow
Another mile to go—but I am dreaming still.

Like Wine

Where the river curved through the valley,
And ferns leaned forward to peep
Cautiously down at their lacy tips,
In pools that were still and deep,
Where spray from a waterfall spattered
In a grey mist silver-starred,
A boy was standing motionless
Like a sentinel on guard.

Had he seen or heard the Leprechaun
Who followed the cobbler's trade,
Or was he rapt in the melody
Of a blackbird's serenade?
Were his eager thoughts of adventure,
Dream castles building on air,
Incited by deeds of gallant men
The heroes who do and dare?

Then I saw the jar, chock-full of bait,
And the rod of crude design.
Had I forgotten the things that go
To a youthful head like wine—
That a chap must always concentrate
When a brown trout holds the line!

Beyond Those Hills

Beyond Maam Cross the friendly hills are waiting,
As sunset streaks the countryside with gold;
Westward we go into the heart of silence,
Children once more returning to the fold.
Beneath the wooded hills, Kylemore is silent,
Only the thrushes singing in the brake;
Here I have walked among the rhododendrons
And watched the shadows deepen on the Lake.

From Letterfrack through Ballinahinch and onwards
I've tried to single out the Pins in vain;
I've watched the fishing boats come in at Cleggan,
And crossed to Innisboffin in the rain.
I've eaten crispy oven bread in Roundstone
And watched the village lads play pitch and toss;
I've talked with gypsies on the road to Cashel
And had my fortune told in Tullycross.

I've listened to the clamour of the shearing,
The bleat of sheep and timid lambs new-shorn,
The rumble of the turf-carts on the cobbles,
The cuckoo's farewell call, faint and forlorn.
I've waited for the salmon fleet at twilight
Through Killary homeward coming with its catch;
I've danced at weddings until dawn was breaking
And rebel songs rang out beneath the thatch.

But I must not stay here idly dreaming
I've got many roads to wander, friends to see,
But first I'll stand and watch the Falls at Aasleagh
And someone from the past might watch with me.

Journeyman Tailor

From Sligo to Ennis I've travelled South
From Ballysodare to the Shannon's mouth.
In a chimney corner many a night
I'd be sitting at peace, my pipe alight,
With the sheep-dog dozing beside my knee
And the crickets chirping away to me
When I was a journeyman tailor.

In summer I'd look for a stack of hay
With birdsong to greet me at break of day.
A carefree man, with no settled abode,
I might take pot-luck on the mountain road
Where Mweelrea stands with her back to the sea
And the stars would kindle their lamps for me
When I was a journeyman tailor.

Northwards on foot, but never a hurry
From Crossmolina to Tubbercurry.
I might get a lift on a jaunting car
From Achill, Manulla or Castlebar,
Discussing the crops as we'd drive along
Or the price of sheep at the fair of Cong
When I was a journeyman tailor.

Through all the five counties my skill was known
From Killary Harbour to Enniscrone.
I've often tramped from Spiddal to Bearna
From Ballyvaughan to Lisdoonvarna.
From the banks of the Moy to Ballymote—
'Tis often I made a swallow-tailed coat
When I was a journeyman tailor.

My needles are rusty, my fingers slow
And few remember how well I could sew.
When a neighbour gives me a simple task
A pipe of tobacco is all I ask.
But most of the time I dwell in the past—
The roads are lonely and I am the last
The last of the journeyman tailors.

Statue in Eyre Square

There, carved in stone, you seem absorbed in thought,
Recording in the music of your words
Some legend sponsored by a fiddler's tune,
The sighing of the wind, the song of birds.

Close by this square in boyhood you explored
Each lamp-lit walk and narrow cobbled street;
You heard the lively clamour of the docks
Or sailed in spirit with the Claddagh fleet.
Beneath the Spanish Arch you often passed,
Or leaned upon a wall beside the weir,
And westward, followed little vagrant roads
That climb between the hills and disappear.

In London's lonely years you made new friends—
Bewildered exiles in an alien land,
Helping at times a weary coster wheel
His apple-barrow through the crowded Strand.
But you remembered rock-encrusted fields
Near Carraroe, and narrow paths that twist
By low stone walls—the fuchsia hedge in bloom,
The herring-boats homecoming through the mist.

Your truant spirit called you back again
To tramp the dusty roads. Contented now,
And unhurried, with ashplant lightly gripped
And careless hat pushed back upon your brow,
Through village street, through market-place or fair,
Threading your way haphazardly among
The restless flock and herds—you talked with men,
Slow-spoken, fluent in their native tongue.

I still can see you on the Spiddal road
Plodding along, heedless of wind and rain,
Or on the way from Cong to Ballinrobe,
Yarning with gypsies in some sheltered lane.

The Music Box

Passing through town at midday, I stopped in a narrow lane,
And pausing outside a window, I peered through a dusty pane.
Within was a motley collection that took my breath away—
Bracelets with rings and broaches laid out on a silver tray;
A cuckoo clock was silent, for the bird had taken flight,
And toby jugs were leering—an unbecoming sight!
A pocket watch of Grandpa's day was anchored to its chain,
A shepherdess in Dresden seemed lost without her swain . . .

I knew I should be moving—right on to Tullamore,
I'm not an art collector but wanted to explore;
In the background I could see a stack of Hogarth prints—
The Rake was making progress at somebody's expense!
I liked the tall brass candlesticks, the little Chinese fan,
The lovely pewter water jug, the copper warming pan;
I saw a stained tobacco-jar, some pottery and ware,
And a locket with a secret I could not hope to share . . .

Then I saw the music-box! In the shop I asked the tune:
A little grey-haired lady said, "'Tis 'The Rising of the Moon'."
I counted all my silver, then reckoned up the score
And listened to my music all the way to Tullamore.

Galway Races

With patience you'll get there, but that's your own affair,
Some take the road before the cock begins to crow;
Around the course to ramble, time to have a gamble,
"Three shots a penny—hit the bull's eye—have a go!"

In we go together and buy a sprig of heather,
Heed the gypsy's warning—the heather must be white;
All ready for the Races, the horses show their paces,
Watch them in the paddock—pick your fancy—pick it right!

The Island men are here, you'd know them anywhere,
Distinctive men are they in famous Aran kit;
In the crowd you cannot miss the pampooties and the *crios*,
Bronzed and sturdy oarsmen on the course at Ballybrit.

Listen to the clatter, the endless chitter-chatter,
All the stalls and 'standings' are doing a thriving trade;
Make your own selection—some delicate confection,
Conversation lozenges or fizzy lemonade!

Up there the owners' stand, trainers on every hand,
Perfume here is wafted with the scent of rich cigars;
The men in deep debate: "What's going to win the Plate?"
The ladies too (God bless 'em all) attired like film stars!

From Kerry and from Clare, from Wexford and Kildare,
Meeting old acquaintances the hours fly by on wings.
It's only once a year and this is what you hear:
"I haven't seen you for a twelvemonth, how are things?"

The horses sleek and smart, all ready for the start;
"Five to one bar one"—hustle and hullabaloo!
They're off without a hitch, over stone wall, over ditch,
Come on there, Number Seven, let's see what you can do!

From Donegal to Cork, and from London to New York,
Of those gala days in Galway people tell,
If you feel laconic, it's better than a tonic,
Set your sails for Galway and Galway's magic spell!

Home Again

In the evening hush as the road led homewards,
Over the valley the mist rode high,
Where the hills were grouped in a friendly circle
Shoulder to shoulder against the sky.
By low stone walls and twisting laneways,
Through wooded hollows where trout streams meet,
I crossed the stile by the briar bushes
Over steps worn smooth by passing feet.

Came the murmur of gaelic softly spoken
As the women prayed by the Holy Well,
The scent of hay from the scythe of the mower,
The distant call of the Vesper bell.
The rowlocks creaked as the fishing curraghs
Steered homewards at dusk to the old grey pier . . .
From byeways clustered with fuchsia blossom
The blackbird's song rang sweet and clear.

*　　*　　*

'Twas the oil-lamp burning low in its bracket,
Lighting the path to the open door,
The spiral of smoke from a cottage chimney,
The white-washed walls, the old stone floor . . .
'Twas the little church with its wooded grotto
That nestled close to the dreaming sea,
And, after Mass, 'twas the smiling faces
Of childhood friends that welcomed me.

Swiftly as though the years slipped backwards,
Blotting out memories of laughter and pain.
'Twas a child once more who heard the greeting:
"God bless you, alanna, you're home again!"

A Shop in the Village

Through the village I went for a reel of white cotton,
I passed the Post Office lettered in green,
I passed the hotel that stood at the corner,
The butcher's, the baker's, the grocer's between!
Then a window I saw that was chock-full of wonder:
There were curranty biscuits and packets of seeds,
There were collar-studs, candles and knots of shoelaces,
There were duck eggs and apples and strings of blue beads!

There was soap, washing soda, hair oil and boot polish,
There were newspapers, comics and wild cowboy tales,
Lemon drops in a bottle, mousetraps and lead pencils,
Fishing flies, walking-sticks, razors and nails.
In the doorway were scythes, reaping-hooks and yard brushes,
From the ceiling hung leggings, galoshes and shoes,
There were onions, potatoes and barrels of herrings,
There were kettles and saucepans—all sizes to choose!

I went into the shop as if drawn by a magnet
And wandered all round with an eager surmise;
I came out with a teapot and jug of blue willow,
A section of honey, a bag of bulls' eyes,
A packet of postcards, a yard of red flannel,
And a model in oak of an old spinning-wheel;
When at home I unloaded my various parcels—
I found I'd forgotton my white cotton reel!

The Bogs of Shanaheever

I heard the music of the fiddle ringing through the gap,
As I was footing turf on a morning in July;
I knew a wedding party was coming through the glen,
And here was I, a carefree lad, spreading turf to dry.

I heard the clang of harness and the beat of horses' hooves,
As side-cars rattled past me, horsemen on either side;
Their laughter filled the valley and they hailed me as they passed,
The fiddler with his fiddle, the bridegroom with his bride.

And far into the mountains I could see them as they rode,
Still heard the beat of horses' hooves, still heard the fiddler play;
'Twas 'The Bogs of Shanaheever', I hummed it wistfully
'Til down the lonely Pass of Maam the music died away.

I stood upon that bog once more (I dared not count the years
Since I had brought the last load home and laid the slane aside);
I listened for the fiddler's tune like the boy of long ago,
But the stretch of bog was silent and not a curlew cried . . .

Then, suddenly and softly, came the music once again,
And though it quickly faded I recognised the theme;
'Twas 'The Bogs of Shanaheever' that the fairy fiddler played,
Sometimes I still can hear it, when I take the time to dream.

The Sycamore

It seemed to peep round the brow of the hill
To welcome me at the gate,
But sadly it rustled each time I left
Heartsick and desolate.
It had knots and knobs and sturdy old roots,
Its bark was peeling and scarred,
But it weathered the storm gallantly
Like a sentinel on guard.

Under the branches the earth was bare,
Trodden down by youthful feet;
Here shelter was sought from the wind and rain
And cover from summer's heat.
Here we played 'shop' with discarded toys,
Sold make-believe tea and bread,
The marks of the swing can still be seen
On that stout branch overhead.

We could scramble out on the thickest branch
As far as the garden wall,
And around the trunk we often carved
Our names in a childish scrawl.
Under this shelter I read of the wolf
With the great big teeth and eyes,
Amazed that Little Red Riding Hood
Was fooled by his thin disguise!

Last week I passed by the brow of the hill,
But the garden was overgrown,
Down by the gate looking weary and bent
The sycamore stood alone . . .

The Churning

By stacks of brown turf that bordered the wayside,
By hillside and hollow, by lake and stone wall,
By green twisting laneways where woodbine was tangled,
I took the short cut for an afternoon call.
Grey spirals of smoke curled up from the cottage
Where thatch upon thatch of the years had been spread,
And I could have told there was soda bread baking
As I walked up the path where the fuchsia was red.

Inviting and cool was the shade of the kitchen,
There was no need to knock at the wide-open door.
My hostess was singing and churning her butter,
The swishing of cream like the waves on the shore.
She was standing erect by her old upright churn,
Her hands plying the dash with wrists supple and strong;
Some cadence of days that were lost and forgotten
Was awakened to life by the lilt of her song.

I helped with the churning—for such was the custom—
And the cups were soon tinkling, the table soon laid;
There was bread from the oven, crisp, hot and melting,
With the butter, fresh salted, Herself had just made.
We sat by the hearth 'til the crickets were chirping,
With the turf fire as high as the smoke blackened crane . . .
There were glow-worms twinkling among the bog cotton
When I took the road home through the green twisting lane.

Road to Anywhere

It's a gathering of the clans
With their tents and caravans,
Goats and donkeys, pots and pans,
Raggle-taggle! Once again
There are gypsies in the lane,
Gypsy Chief and all his train.

Sheltered underneath the trees
Camps are pitched with practised ease,
Wood fires crackle in the breeze;
Something's cooking over there,
Caught this morning in a snare—
(Little bunnies, do beware!)

Gypsy women, brown and bold,
Flash their ear-rings, hoops of gold,
"Lady, want your fortune told?
Tall and fair and handsome he
From a land beyond the sea
Coming in the space of three!"

Breaking through the evening hush
Comes the song of mating thrush,
Nestling in the hawthorn bush.
By the camp-fire in the shade
Ukelele softly played,
'Tis a gypsy serenade.

In a caravan close by
Brown-eyed babies sleeping lie
To a gypsy lullaby.
Life goes on without a care,
Off to market, off to fair,
On the road to anywhere . . .

The Travelling Man

"'Twas a lonely road," said the travelling man,
"No one to greet me there.
No smoke in the hollow, no cross roads dance,
No threecard trick at the fair.

"There were students conversing in Spiddal,
There were artists in Carraroe,
There were boys grooming ponies in Clifden
In trim for the Pony Show.

"Then I thought of the past, the roadside camp,
Of the rabbits I snared and sold,
Of the kettles and pots my father fixed,
Of the fortunes my mother told.

"Tonight I'll sleep by the road to Leenane
And awaken at dawn's first glow.
It's a downhill road by the Killaries
But a journey that I must go.

"For the roads of Mayo are calling to me
From Roonah, Old Head, Achill Sound,
When the harvest moon looks over Clew Bay
I hope I'll still be around".

March Comes In

Beyond the mists that blanketed Slea Head,
A hooker by the Blaskets showed her dusky sail;
I saw a woman milking cows beside her door,
The milk with frothy whiteness brimmed her pail.
When she had guided me upon my way, she said:
"The winds of March are stirring up in Dingle Bay,
The clouds are gathering fast along the Head,
God bless you, and God speed you on your way!"

A farmer drove his harrow through a field near Patrick's Well.
"It's time the weather favoured us—we should be planting now."
The ghost of last year's scarecrow still flapped its tattered coat
Beside a ridge where brown earth lay, upturned by the plough.

A shepherd walked with me a while 'twixt Foxford and Pontoon,
Keeping a watchful eye betimes upon his wayward sheep.
"One March", he told me sadly, with bitter memory,
"I lost my lambs, new born, when drifts of snow lay deep!"

A worker on a roadway that led to Sligo town,
When sleet was driving coldly, led me to shelter nigh.
He pointed out the region where Drumcliffe Churchyard lay—
Then round by steep Ben Bulben I heard the March winds sigh.

An artist mixed his colours near the woods by Kylemore Pass,
The brush upon his palette creating light and shade;
The noonday sky was overcast, and on his easel showed
The dark uneasy shadows the drifting clouds had made.

A fisherman with gnarled hands repaired his broken nets,
Outside his whitewashed cottage, heedless of wind and rain.
"For salmon on the Killary I've fished for thirty years,
Our luck has varied—whose has not—thank God we can't complain".

A gypsy lazed beside his camp upon the Spiddal road,
He hailed me with a shout as I went by;
I marvelled at his colouring—the brown of sun and wind—
Alert and gaily twinkling his bright eyes searched the sky.
"For the rain", he cried, "I care not, or bitter winds of March,
If I can snare a rabbit and my canvas keeps me dry;
We'll have summer by the wayside when we take the road for Tuam
We'll have fun at Galway Races in July."

Fishermen All

I heard the creaking of heavy boots
As they shuffled across the floor,
When the priest called out from the pulpit
"Move up you boys from the door!"
Then he turned the page of his Gospel
And seemed occupied with the text,
But all the time I knew that his eye
Was on me as well as the next!
"It's a great day indeed for the anglers
But you won't be long delayed,
There are empty pews up here in front"—
and we sheepishly obeyed,
With a thought (that surely God would forgive)
Of the river alive with trout,
A hasty snack when the prayers were said
And good luck to the first man out!

John Larry was there from the Glenside,
Hook-nosed and lean as a goat;
I had to smile at the scrap of wool
That clung to his Sunday coat!
I saw big Paddy the carpenter
and Danny, known as the 'Vet';
No fancy letters after his name
But the best cow-doctor yet.
The tailor was clad in a smart new suit,
Looking quite neat and spry,
But not a stitch in that tweed of mine
That I gave him last July!
Peter the postman you'd hardly know
Dressed up in his Sunday best;
Under the pulpit three limbs of the Law
Were sitting sedately abreast.

Parted awhile from hammer and last
Was little cobbler Shawn,
(Every time I look at that man
I think of a Leprechaun . . .)
The teacher was facing the organ,
The choir at her back in a row,
The doctor was there, and the man in grey
Back home from Idaho.
Each man of them was a fisherman
Or aspired to be one at least,
But I'd lay a bet that none of them
Could handle a rod like the priest!
Was there a hope in the back of his mind
(And if so it wasn't a crime)
That he might get there ahead of them
If they'd only take their time?

"It's a great day indeed for the anglers,
And you're all in a hurry no doubt.
You'll soon be down by the river bank
Having a go at the trout.
But when the service is over,
Don't make such a rush, I implore.
I'll ask you to walk in a seemly way
One by one towards the door!"

Echoes

Down through the glen the music was ringing,
Louder it swelled as I faced the steep climb.
'Twas the fiddler from Inagh: I knew he was tapping
One foot on the floor to help him keep time.

Under the thatch the couples were dancing
'Til the cups that hung on the dresser danced too;
In the path of the lamplight a young rabbit scuttled
And two bearded goats in a twinkling withdrew.

Bold rebel songs rang out through the glenside,
Silver-cloaked in the light of the Harvest moon.
From Recess to Renvyle and the white sands of Omey
They came, and they danced to the fiddler's tune.

*   *   *

Years have not changed the hills or the heather,
Or the lazy old river's gossiping tone,
Or the song of the thrush as it rings through the coppice,
But I am a stranger walking alone.

Down through the glen faint music comes stealing,
Grows louder, then flutters to silence once more . . .
Over years long forgotten an echo has sounded—
Lost notes that only a dream can restore.

Home Town

I knew the short cut: it led down through the field
Where the mushrooms grew thick long ago,
Led out by a laneway that skirted a bog
Towards the village that huddled below.
The Angelus rang from the low-steepled church,
And I counted the strokes as they came;
'Twas a custom of childhood—and memory leaped
Through each solemn note like a flame.

The street did not seem quite as wide as of yore
And the houses not nearly so high;
(I remember the time when the trees were so tall
Their tips brushed the stars in the sky!)
I passed by the pump, unpretentious and squat,
By the signpost that creaked in the breeze;
Young and shrill rang the voices of children at school
Unburdened with care and unease.

I came to the corner, and found it still there
Just the same as of old, just as grand.
The shop where I squandered my few hoarded pence
Clutched hot in the palm of my hand.
In the window were dolls, some blonde and well groomed,
Some brunettes, to be handled with care,
But they could not surpass their ancestors of old,
That once I had coveted there.

A family of ducks had invaded the green,
A horse slaked his thirst in the pond;
I passed the post office, the modest town hall,
And the meadows unfolded beyond.
Then . . . softly each outline grew shapeless and blurred,
And I groped with a puzzled surprise;
'Til I woke to the sound of a city's new day
With the tears of a dream in my eyes.

That Man of Mine

We strolled together through Montmartre,
We climbed the Eiffel Tower;
Inspired with reverence and awe,
The treasures of the Louvre we saw,
And lived each magic hour.

At famed Maxim's we dined in state
One gay bewitching night;
The pavement cafés we explored
And, sipping coffee, much deplored
Our holiday's swift flight.

One morning on the boulevards
Some imp of mischief stirred,
And whispered to that man of mine
The price of cattle would decline—
I vowed it was absurd!

One afternoon in royal Versailles
And much to my dismay,
He questioned me: "Are you aware
That I have missed the autumn fair
In Ballinasloe today?"

That man of mine became a bore
He found the Follies dull,
He worked out budgets in his sleep,
Had dreams about the price of sheep
And nightmares about wool!

*　　*　　*

We're back again in Donegal
And everything is fine.
Enchanting city far away
I'll visit you again some day
Without that man of mine!

As You and I Remember

When the train steamed in with its whistle blowing
To that tiny station, lamp-lit and dim . . .
When the porter shouted "A merry Chirstmas",
And we shouted the same wish back to him . . .
When the roofs were white and the trees snow-laden
Just like the scene on a Christmas card . . .
When the side-car bumped as it turned each corner
And the countryside was freezing hard . . .
When the lamps were lighting in every window
And a snowman squatted behind the gate . . .
When log fires blazed and holly glistened
And tall red candles stood in state . . .
When the pool was frozen beyond the meadow
And the hills resembled a painted scene—
I think of all this when it comes to Christmas,
Forgetting the years that have passed between.

When the glorious whiff of sage and onion
Seeped through the kitchen and filled the air,
And the crackling came from the fireside oven—
No need to be told that the goose was there!
When the old house echoed to peals of laughter
And snowflakes came in a whirling shower,
Old songs were sung and old tales remembered
Long, long after the midnight hour;
'Til the lamps burned low and the candles flickered
And the hallowed night had grown serene . . .
I think of all this when I think of Christmas
Forgetting the years that have passed between.

The Kitchen Dresser

It had stood there for years, shelves scrubbed almost white
By hands slim and youthful, by hands weary and old.
It had welcomed each coming and witnessed each going,
And stood there unmoved with its story untold.

On top were some letters from faraway places
Often read and reread, then answered with care,
To those who remembered, but might never return
To that wayside cottage near Ballysodare.

Two blue willow dishes leaned over the cross-beam,
The plates overlapped on a shelf of their own;
The jugs stood together, some tall and some buxom,
But an earthenware teapot stood proudly alone.

Cups and saucers in plenty and eggcups upstanding,
Half-a-dozen chipped mugs bore nursery rhymes.
Poor Little Miss Muffet and Old Mother Hubbard
Had clearly been fashioned in far better times.

             ★   ★   ★

She sat by the fireside, her hands busy knitting,
The turf burning brightly, the hearth-stone swept clean.
In the flickering firelight she told me her story,
While she wound up the wool and I held the skein.

As she moved through the kitchen, her voice was now silent,
Her thoughts of the past, where I could not intrude;
But the tea that she poured from her earthenware teapot
Was surely the finest that ever was brewed.

They Will Remember

Through crowded streets ablaze with festive lights
Lonely they'll walk in their adopted land
Dreaming of home and cherished days of youth
Like shipwrecked sailors on a foreign strand.

Will they perhaps recall some long lost tune
Once softly played within the firelight's glow,
Or see the flicker of a candle's gleam
On cobbled streets, footprinted in the snow?

Will they remember landmarks of their youth
Broad fields of wheat by roadsides in Kildare
A salmon leaping in a Galway lake
A blackbird whistling in a Dublin square?

Will they recall the Shannon at Athlone
The Kerry Coast, peaks misty in the dawn
The Barrow and the Suir, the lovely Lee
The Wicklow hills in sheltered peace withdrawn?

Such pictures once were fresh in memory's frame
Until the veil of years was overcast;
But wistfully each one will try to fill
Parts missing from the jig-saw of the past.

Around the hearth we'll gently speak their names,
And faces in the fire will slowly form;
May God be with them in each land they dwell
And keep them safe in sunshine and in storm.

By Lagan Banks

I walked along the Antrim road, the house was still the same,
Except that no one living there would recognise my name.
No wrinkles marked the smoothness of that solid red brick face,
The drapes, in sober colours, hung rigidly in place,
The door was newly painted, the big brass knocker shone
Unchanged through generations that must have come and gone.

I looked for Smithfield Market, beyond Shankill and Falls,
The folks who once belonged there among their booths and stalls.
I missed the bargain hunters, the buyers and the sellers,
Organ-grinders, wheeler dealers, fiddlers, fortune-tellers,
The ceaseless hum of barter, hard bargains driven there,
The ready wit and laughter, the kinship of the fair.

I tried to think of place names and some eluded me,
But some were unforgotten, for each held a memory:
The lovely Glens of Antrim, wrapped in the twilight hush,
The mysteries of the Causeway, the sand banks of Portrush,
I walked along the Lagan that evening in the rain
And felt a sense of something lost I could not now regain.

But, clearer than all others was that day in late July,
Leaning from a carriage window, my good friends standing by,
The last farewells, the promises, the parting of the ways.
Would I recognise them now, after all those yesterdays?
Last night, outside the City Hall, I watched the traffic flow
As I had watched it that first night, some fifty years ago.

Mother City

Were I far from her friendly shelter,
Of these would my memories be:
The steep winding road to the mountains,
The blackbird's song in Glencree;
The Sugar Loaf, hunched up and dozing
Beneath a mist-blanket of grey;
The beacon at Kish ever flashing
Its message far out in the Bay . . .

Howth Head, purple-gowned in the autumn
With a tang of salt in the air;
Killiney Bay drowsing in moonlight—
Was there ever a scene so fair?

The Castle, dark-browed and reflective,
The Four Courts of storied renown,
And streets of a past generation
Where stately old mansions look down . . .
The bustle of life by the river,
The prow of an oncoming boat,
Swans gracefully breasting the current,
The Custom House standing remote.

The sound of the city would echo
Like a song with a wistful theme,
And I'd walk on her old grey pavements
In the shadowed light of a dream.

The Bridge of Sighs

They'll surely be the death of me—
Blackwood, Stayman and Acol.
Just one alone can scare me stiff
But three I couldn't tackle!
The weak take-out bamboozles me,
The end-play squeeze, the double jump,
The opening three that's Greek to me,
The strong and weak no-trump.

I count my points like a kid at school,
The total is never the same.
Why do the others glare at me?
Am I holding up the game?
One for a Jack, two for a Queen,
Add on the King and the Ace;
Have I a void, a singleton?
Please! Please! a moment's grace!

I look around in mute appeal
Like a stranger lost in a crowd.
"There is no need", my partner scowls,
"To count your points aloud."
It looks as if I can't escape,
I must bid at any cost;
I settle for the little slam
And keep my fingers crossed.

By strange finesse and lucky guess
I made the slam, thank Heaven!
My partner scowled at me again,
"You should have made the seven!"

The Elusive One

You have travelled round the world, alert and fancy-free,
From Rio de Janeiro to the Island of Capri.
In many a far-flung city you've caused a hue and cry,
On many a lonely island from the Solomons to Skye.
You've blazed your way through frontiers, you've cruised the Seven Seas,
You've been hailed in every language from Dutch to Portuguese.
From Cuba to the Cameroons there's tribute paid to you
From London to Kentucky and from Sydney to Peru!

You've been sought in every quarter from Quebec to Singapore,
You've been guarded like a treasure from New York to Labrador;
You've got suitors in Vancouver, you've got rendezvous in Spain,
And through the Windy City you've been toasted in champagne!
You've been lost in San Francisco, you've been found in Aberdeen,
You're full of whims and fancies but you're treated like a queen!
This time I've got a feeling that you'll crown me with success—
Oh, my Irish Sweepstake girl, take a note of my address!

For Sale—and Wanted

For Sale
A stately home in Tudor style approached by carriage-ways
Where coachmen drove equipages in long-forgotten days;
Far, far removed from dust and smoke of crowded factory towns,
Tall windows that disclose a view of undulating downs;
A paddock and a tennis court, yachts moored beside the pier,
A lake's exclusive fishing rights, a woodland stocked with deer.

A ballroom and a library, a cellar of choice wine,
A banquet-hall where epicures by candlelight may dine.

Wanted
A three-roomed house among the hills, beside the water's edge,
Its brick-red chimneys peeping out above a fuchsia hedge;
Four white-washed walls, an open hearth, a stack of turf bone dry,
The murmur of a mountain stream that tumbles closely by;
Grey seagulls circling round the cliffs, crying hoarsely in their flight,
A curragh moored beyond the Point, sea-worthy, feather-light.

A garden, wild with buttercups, where I can sit and dream,
A midnight meal by candlelight with brown trout from the stream!

Lot Twenty-Nine

I wandered through an auction room
Crammed up with strangest things:
Pianos, carpets, sewing-machines,
Decanters, teapots, soup tureens,
And silver napkin rings.
I saw an old grandfather clock,
Its pendulum at rest,
A bronze athlete of long ago,
His discus ready for the throw,
Poised on an oaken chest.

A pair of tongs with lengthy limbs,
A battered leather bellows;
'Mid thrillers, yellow-backed and gay,
Dog-eared and wistful Shakespeare lay
Amid his strange bed-fellows.
I saw a group of chessmen too
Bearing their battle scars;
Saw china, glass and statuettes,
With Queen Anne chairs and cabinets
And old tobacco jars.

A regal sideboard finely carved
Seemed made of sterner stuff;
I wondered what its life had been:
Had it seen hoop and crinoline
And dandies taking snuff?
A wicker chair like Granny's own
(that used to groan and creak),
Those candlesticks, with snuffers too,
Those brass affairs, for all I knew
Were probably antique!

And then I saw him leer at me
In manner bold and crude
With bulbous nose and toothy grin,
A wart upon his ample chin,
His ugly face upscrewed!
Lot twenty-nine consisted of
A tarnished christening mug,
A carving knife, some broken delph—
And with them all I got Himself,
That grinning Toby Jug!

Brain Child

I wrote it in an attic
    Some seven storeys high.
Remote and dedicated,
Ideas radiated
    As summer drifted by.

Above the city clamour,
    Alone and undisturbed,
I analysed, dissected,
I moulded and rejected
    Debating every word.

I polished it and pruned it
    Behind the fire-escape;
I trimmed it and revised it,
Admired it, yet despised it,
    But coaxed it into shape.

I finished it one morning
    Alone in my retreat,
When all the world was sleeping
And dawn's cold wind was sweeping
    Across the empty street.

Then, afterwards surrounded
    By half-smoked cigarettes,
I crumpled, in dejection,
That brief note of rejection:
    "The Editor regrets . . ."

The Old House

It's little changed since yesterday—
This house that I had always known—
The monkey-puzzle tree close by,
That once was scarcely shoulder high,
Now almost to the roof has grown.

'Twas here that I found sanctuary
From simple troubles, childhood fears,
Within those walls no danger pressed
And no anxiety distressed
The carefree hours of youthful years.

I must not venture near that door.
How could I boldly thus intrude?
What stumbling questions could I frame
When no one there might speak my name
Or know of my solicitude?

I'd like to steal inside just once
And tiptoe softly through each room,
Then lean far out the window-sill
To see the gorse upon the hill,
The lilac trees in early bloom.

I'd like to wander through the fields
Where once the scarecrow stood, and see
The old stone wall where ivy clings,
The thicket where the blackbird sings,
The names we carved upon a tree!

I shall not often pass that door
And time may teach me to forget!
Through all the years that come and go
'Twill bring me comfort just to know
Those sturdy walls are standing yet.

Where I Belong

Our little place is full of cheer,
Just something in the atmosphere;
And I go there each year to see
The members of my family tree.
The village pump—it creaks and creaks,
The village clock has stopped for weeks;
I love it still, don't get me wrong,
This little place where I belong!

One man gets fat and one gets lean
And others stop halfway between;
That old, old boy is my Grandpa,
He's older than Methuselah.
From time to time the horses neigh,
They sometimes feel the need of hay;
The sheep don't know they've got to die
They've never heard of Shepherds Pie!

The village shop has pots and pails,
Has hooks and eyes and coffin nails,
Has mousetraps, cheese and sennapods,
Has acid drops and fishing-rods.
All day the village cats miaow,
The dogs create an awful row.
O'Leary's ducks are on the loose
Heading them off—Mullarky's goose!

The pub is open awfully late,
The barmaid's name is Mary Kate,
The village cop is on his beat
Stamping along on two fine feet . . .
Oh, come and see my old Grandpa,
The bingo in the cinema,
The pub that's open awfully late,
The village cop and Mary Kate!

The village pump—it creaks and creaks,
The village clock has stopped for weeks;
I love it still, don't get me wrong
This little place where I belong!

The Connemara Bus

It comes with a hoot through the village street;
"Is there any chance of a vacant seat?"
"There might be now—take the weight off your feet"
On the Connemara Bus!

You'll get to Galway whatever befalls,
Twisting and turning by low stone walls,
And the women will wear their woolly shawls
On the Connemara Bus!

Baskets of eggs will be up on the rack,
And you'll hear the ducks as they quack, quack, quack,
Their yellow beaks sticking out of a sack
On the Connemara Bus!

You'd certainly know it was Market Day
With the chickens chirping all the way,
And we talk about prices as we sway
On the Connemara Bus!

The journey would surely be worth your while
For the yarns in Gaelic would make you smile;
The women discussing the latest style
On the Connemara Bus!

To the city of Galway once a week
It's a great excursion, so to speak,
For the atmosphere is most unique
On the Connemara Bus!

To all newcomers we smile and we nod,
(Make room for the chap with the fishing rod)
"Tis a grand soft day and thanks be to God"
On the Connemara Bus!

Pass the Meringues

Because you're somewhat overweight
And anxious to reduce,
At breakfast time you play around
With toast and orange juice . . .
Let me have bacon fried with egg
To usher in the day,
Let me have tea and marmalade
Upon my breakfast tray.
For lunch I like a juicy steak
Well flanked with golden chips,
I do not mind the extra curve
Thus added to my hips!
I like a lobster mayonnaise,
An apple dumpling too,
In fact I'm fond of everything
You say I should eschew!
You vow it's just plain greediness
And much deplore my taste
(I'm heading for a double chin,
A crazy mixed-up waist!)
You nibble at a lettuce leaf
To keep your waist line in,
Please pass me over those meringues—
I'll chance the double chin!

Fragments

You'll find them huddled in a trunk
Or anywhere amid the junk,
And leisure hours will swiftly fly
As you regard them with a sigh—
Those fragments of the years gone by.
This album full of childish scrawls
Some youthful incident recalls;
That schoolbook of the long ago
Falls open where the pages show
Those verses that you used to know.

Those colours of your favourite team
'Mid old forgotten trophies gleam,
Rosettes once gay, maroon and white,
Reluctant to confront the light,
Enjoyed at least one gala night.
A theatre programme, date unknown,
Its gilded edges tarnished grown,
Brings back tonight some far-off stage;
Those names upon the cardboard page
Are faint and yellowed now with age.

An ancient diary little used,
Some coloured crayons much abused;
Within a ragged wallet's fold,
A tiny card with printing bold
Your fortune and your weight had told.
Some rusty keys upon a ring,
A set of draughts, a violin string,
Stamps, hoarded once with loving care,
Newspaper cuttings in a layer,
A host of snapshots everywhere.

The jigsaw puzzle you retrieve,
The pattern once again you weave,
That invitation to a dance,
That picture postcard sent from France—
You'll see their purport at a glance.
You'll find them huddled in a trunk
Or anywhere amid the junk,
And through you threaten, never fear.
Long years from now they'll still be there,
Those souvenirs of yesteryear.

Best Laid Schemes

September, October, when autumn is speeding,
I'm already computing the cash I'll be needing
If I go for a holiday next year to Spain.
There's much to be said for an early decision
Which may be subjected to later revision,
Last-minute adjustments are often in vain!

November, December, during bleak wintry times,
In my dreams I'm already in tropical climes,
Away from the east wind, the frost and the rain.
There's Lugano, Capri and there's lovely Lucerne,
I ponder them over with thoughtful concern
Assessing their merits again and again.

January, February, when spring is awaking,
I'm planning the route I'll surely be taking
By luxury liner, by car or by plane!

In March and in April the first doubts assail me
That my slender resources will scarcely avail me,
That my roving ambitions have soared a bit high.
I add and subtract with a grim concentration,
Deploring the cost of a simple vacation,
It's amazing how swiftly your savings can fly!

In May and in June I'm right back where I started,
The problem is worse and I'm getting downhearted
For holiday time is so quickly drawing nigh . . .
There's a place in the country which might be propitious
What a pity I left it too late to apply!

As July steals upon me all hopes disappear,
In August I'm dreaming again of next year
And laying out new plans of campaign with a sigh!

Builders and Providers

In the airy world of feathers, preparations are in swing;
Housing is the main objective of all families in spring.
Pigeons coo and blackbirds whistle, thrushes fill the woods with song;
Sparrows, bustling in the chimneys, chitter-chatter all day long.

Rooks keep snooping round the furrows, wary eyes upon the seeds,
Water-hens, like busy housewives, fetch and carry through the reeds.
Jenny wren, an expert builder, makes her little home secure,
Lapwings circle through the marshes, curlews call across the moor.

Little robins plan and potter, quarrelsome beyond belief,
What a hoarder is the jackdaw, he's a plain and simple thief!
Cuckoo senior, good-for-nothing, never builds himself a nest,
Cuckoo junior, cocky youngster, is a most ill-mannered guest.

Members of each feathered family hustle with their own affairs,
In their black and white ensemble magpies gossiping in pairs.
As the plough upturns the furrow, greedy gulls appear in sight,
All the hungry worm hunters swooping for a juicy bite!

How the scarecrow looks forbidding, clad in rags of rusty black,
But he won't make much impression on that noisy squabbling pack;
Some will perch upon his shoulder—cheeky fellows—just to show
Man must think up something better if he wants to scare a crow!

The Schoolroom Dance

Do you remember long ago the fiddler in the school,
Smiling as he fiddled crouched there upon his stool,
Refreshed at seemly intervals by drinks of something cool?
No tune in all our repertoire that fiddler couldn't play,
And each demand we made of him it pleased him to obey
Without a word of protest or a moment of delay!

We had supper in the classroom 'mid desks we used to know,
The ball-frame near the window with its marbles in a row,
The blackboard on the easel—Oh! shades of long ago!

The lamplight flickered faintly as the hours went flitting by,
'Til the fiddler packed his fiddle when the dawn was in the sky
And on our way reluctantly we wandered with a sigh.

By a bridge that spanned the river where the mists of morning lay,
By the laneways where the thrushes sang their welcome to the day,
By the hedgerows and the woodlands we sauntered on our way . . .

A smart and gleaming omnibus, from stem to stern alight,
Now duly runs to schedule past the crossroads every night,
But the little fragrant laneways are hidden far from sight!

On dance occasions nowadays the village simply hums;
To a brand new hall in Main Street a splendid dance band comes—
In a haughty station-wagon—with saxophones and drums!
As on the shining instruments the street lamps softly glow,
My memory seeks the fiddler in the school I used to know,
As dreamily he played for us those tunes of long ago!

The Ruthless One

What man is this who strides along
With grim determination,
Nor looks to left, nor looks to right,
Nor finds in any rustic sight
New charms of creation?

How wild his eyes, how strange his guise,
How purposeful his jaw!
I do not like that smile of his,
A criminal he surely is
Escaping from the Law!

The lambs are startled by his tread
And timidly retreat;
The snowdrops with their drooping heads,
The violets peeping from their beds
Are crushed beneath his feet.

It's possible he does not hear
The thrush and blackbird sing.
He's not impressed by blossom-time
For he's more occupied with crime
Than with the voice of spring.

There's something sinister afoot,
And I must do my part;
So, even though my senses reel,
I'll trail him swiftly, for I feel
There's murder in his heart.

But when I saw the weapon raised
Stark horror struck me chill;
'Twas just as well I didn't shout
For soon I saw a golden trout
Being landed for the kill!

Interlude

She chewed her gum in Merrion Square
With a roving eye and a jaunty air;
Bus number eight came swinging along,
She and her chewing gum both got on.
To the upper deck I heard her climb,
Her high heels clicked and her jaws kept time,
Planked herself down on a seat near me,
Told me she came from Tennessee.
As her accent filled the tall green bus
To Tennessee went all of us!

In her auto we whirled through USA
(I guess we were simply carried away)
From Kennedy in a Boeing plane
Over to Shannon, swimming in rain,
Hung by our heels towards the Blarney stone,
Crossed the historic Bridge of Athlone . . .
Then suddenly our jaws began
Revolving in rhythm from man to man,
We chewed and chewed in that tall green bus
Till the checker came and chewed with us.

Meantime we looked through the Book of Kells,
Listened awhile to the Shandon Bells,
Flew over once more with Alcock and Browne
And landed safely near Clifden Town.
After all this she waved us goodbye
With her Tennessee smile and her roving eye.
We watched her crossing another square,
Chewing her gum with a nonchalant air . . .
We were silent now on that tall green bus
Wishing her well in the hearts of us.

Aftermath

Vacation sadly over
You're home from fields of clover,
And on your threshold hover
With memories that reach
Way back to starlit places,
Blue skies and open spaces,
Or laughing sun-bronzed faces
Upon some crowded beach!

How came this room so musty,
The furniture so dusty,
With spiders grown so lusty,
Spinning their webs of grey?
How came that plant so weary,
Those curtains drab and dreary,
That once were bright and cheery
Before you sailed away?

The kitchen looks neglected,
Milk bottles uncollected,
Forlorn and dejected,
And in so short a time!
With visions of housekeeping,
Of polishing and sweeping,
You're on the verge of weeping
(Last week was so sublime!)

New hope and courage muster!
Arise and get your duster
And wake the bygone lustre
That has so swiftly flown...
No time to waste on brooding
Though mem'ry keeps intruding
I'll bet that you're concluding
There's no place like your own!

What's My Line?

Tales of mystery and detection with a multitude of clues,
Lurid books in gaudy jackets such as *Murder in the Mews*:
Such has been my reading-matter—but indeed it's nearly time
That I aimed at something bigger and gave up this life of crime!

My neglected education is a fact I much deplore,
There are avenues of knowledge that I might well explore,
So I linger in the library and wonder what's my line;
I must organise my reading to follow some design.

Could I specialise in Classics and study for degrees?
Perhaps I'd find my *métier* in French or Portuguese?
Mythology? Astrology—the shape of things to be?
Geology? Biology? Psychology? *Not me!*

I seek among the bookshelves for something less obscure:
Political Economy I simply can't endure,
I feel no urge towards History, Biography, or Law,
I'd be addled by the genius of Shakespeare or of Shaw!

Then suddenly I make my choice and beat a quick retreat,
I hasten through the library and now I'm in the street;
Away with all this highbrow stuff! It's far beyond my range
I've picked another thriller—bound in yellow for a change!

Quarantine

I've read all the papers line by line,
I've followed the astronauts;
I've dwelt for a while in outward space.
Rocketing back to the self-same place,
And trying to collect my thoughts.

I've read news items from far and near,
I've noted the racing tips;
I've learned the trend of the latest style
And I've smiled a wan and sickly smile
At the usual comic strips.

I've browsed through all the market reports,
Textiles, tobaccos and mines;
I know the prices at Billingsgate
Of halibut, haddock, prawns and skate,
I've followed the shipping lines.

I know how to banish freckles and spots,
How to coax back vanished hair,
How to attack in a game of chess,
How to succeed in a bridge finesse,
How to cover an armchair!

I've studied the films, glanced at the shows,
I've yawned through the book reviews;
I've read the forecasts of storm and rain
And, rousing up my somnolent brain,
I've delved into crossword clues.

And now I'm reading between the lines,
As they say shrewd readers do
(Knock, knock! Bang, bang! So there's no one there?
Of course, they've left, for I'm like a bear)
Did they tell you? I've got 'flu!

Plum Pudding

Grate those breadcrumbs, grate them finely,
Fourteen ounces, no excess.
One half lb. of flour, self-raising,
(Have you scales or do you guess?).
Use a lb. of Demerara,
More or less, it's up to you.
Raisins, currants and sultanas—
Just a lb. of each will do.

(Make a mess, the same as I do,
Drop your litter on the floor;
If the butcher's boy is calling,
Don't go rushing to the door!)

Take a quarter lb. of cherries,
Apples, two, please chop or dice,
Grate your orange skin and lemon,
Add a teaspoonful of spice.
Use a quarter of chopped almonds
And the same of muscatels,
Candied peel—about eight ounces,
Nine good eggs—without the shells!

(Take a peep around the kitchen,
Anything else you might include?
Use the orange juice and lemon,
But omit the baby's food!)

Ounces, twelve, of suet or butter,
Add a pinch or two of salt,
Grated carrot, grated nutmeg,
Last, not least, a glass of malt!
Maybe whiskey, maybe brandy,
But I'll cast my vote for rum;
Is there anything I've omitted
From this pudding—but the plum?

(Other flavours may be added,
You must let your fancy roam;
Tie it in a pudding-basin
Boil it 'til the cows come home!)

Profit or Loss?

I have heard some passengers discuss
Their holidays on a crowded bus.
Yesterday, on a number seven,
I learnt that Paris is simply heaven.
"We drove to the vineyards of sunny France
To a city pulsing with romance."
I was lucky to thumb a wagon-ride
With empties rattling by my side
Through places I fear you wouldn't know
From Lisdoonvarna to Ballinasloe.
"Les dames de Paris are simply divine,
The food delicious and also the wine."
Give me trout from the mountain stream
Then a blackberry tart with lots of cream.
"The crowds were gay on the boulevards."
The kitchen for me and a game of cards!
"When I came home I hadn't a sou—
Life will be bleak for a month or two."
Next year you should try the open spaces
I showed a profit at Galway Races.

A Place in the Country

Through his books went the agent in rapid survey,
"You're seeking a place in the country, you say?
Much depends, I assure you, on what you can pay!
I take it your aim is a house near the city,
Framed in a setting of rustic serenity!
Yet equipped with every social amenity?
Here's something to suit you", he quickly decided,
"A house with all modern comforts provided,
Electrical fittings throughout", he confided.

(He was trying to be helpful but how could he tell
That I wanted to carry my pail from the well,
By a path through the woods as twilight fell?
I wanted a white-washed house of my own
With a big turf fire on the wide hearthstone,
And the crickets singing to me alone!
The sun's last rays on the straw of the thatch,
A rabbit astir in the cabbage patch,
That answering click in the spring of the latch!)

As my wayward thoughts on their wanderings sped:
"It's newly papered and painted", he said,
"There's a garage, a greenhouse and gardening shed.
It is semi-detached", he went on to relate,
"Gabled and shuttered and most up-to-date,
With an excellent bus service right at your gate.
Labour-saving devices are much to the fore,
With built-in presses and cupboards galore,
And useful recesses you'll simply adore!"

(Sure I'd make me a besom and tie it with string,
From a line in the haggard my washing would swing,
And I'd dust out my room with a grey goose's wing!
I'd have speckled brown trout from the dark mountain stream,
My little chipped crock would be brimming with cream
And my mushrooms I'd cook by the candlelight's gleam.
I'd have buttermilk cool from my earthenware urn,
In the cinders big floury potatoes would burn,
With butter awaiting them fresh from the churn!)

As I dreamt of the land where my fancy had flown,
Impatient—no wonder—the agent had grown,
So I managed to say in a faltering tone:
"But I'm looking for hills where the trout streams glide,
Where the blackbird lilts in the eventide,
And I want stone walls where the west winds bide!"
"Stone walls!", he exclaimed, "and the blackbird's song,
Faith—there's many a road you can travel along,
Try you luck by the Rosses, the Slaney or Cong!"

Night Out

Cigarette smoke in a dense blue haze
Spirals aloft to the ceiling;
Hail fellow-well-met, you smile as you pass,
The popping of corks and tinkle of glass
Awakens a kindred feeling.

It's a cold, cold night and there's snow outside,
You could do with a nice hot rum;
As the liquor flows like fire through your veins
You realise you have plenty of brains—
That the others are just plain dumb!

You're the life of the party very soon,
Your voice grows louder and bolder,
Your neighbour, a stranger, tells you his woes,
You buy him a drink as the tempo grows
And he weeps, perhaps, on your shoulder.

Those income tax people have got you down
You're certainly going to fight 'em;
The country is finished without a doubt—
No wonder the people are clearing out—
And so on—ad infinitum.

"Time, Gentlemen, please!" and you're soon outside,
Farewells are spoken with sorrow;
Just people you met in a crowded bar
And you won't have an earthly who they are
Should they cross your path tomorrow.

Staggering home—you're telling yourself
How you'd fix the United Nations,
But your fluent tongue is a weight of lead—
In fact you haven't a tongue in your head
When it comes to Home Relations.

Mushroom Year 1949

There were miners, forty-niners, headlong in their rush for gold,
We saw other forty-niners, just as keen, if truth were told.
Armed with every kind of vessel, eyes alert upon their prey,
Hedge-tears, scratches, all forgotten, for the hunt brooks no delay!
Little creamy mushrooms sprouting—adults in a single night,
Full-blown beauties, helmets drooping, how they whet the appetite.
Lined with palest pink perfection, springing up on every hand
(And the farmer made no protest when we trespassed on his land!)

You might try them out with salmon cutlets: such a dish is but a dream,
Or with brown trout fresh and sparkling from the dark pools of the
    stream.
They're delicious fried in butter, served with bacon, kidney, toast,
Adding lustre to a chicken or a tender juicy roast.
Mushrooms stewed in creamy splendour such delicious morsels make,
Or golden buttons coyly cuddling in the shelter of a steak.
Mushroom sauce for many dishes all its appetising self,
Mushroom ketchup stored in bottles high upon the pantry shelf.

Jars of mushrooms neatly labelled, culled from lowlands far and near,
Not for long to stay in storage—soon they too will disappear . . .
Every time we taste their flavour, we remember days of old
When we crossed the farmer's hedges—patient man, he didn't scold!
Gather round the fire at sundown, mushrooms sizzle on the sods,
In their cups the bright juice bubbling, sure it's nectar for the gods,
When an omelette, wrapped in mushrooms, welcomes me at twilight
    late,
For caviare, a fig I care not, garnished on a golden plate!

Hurdy-Gurdy

Listen to the hurdy-gurdy
As you wander through the fair,
Take a peep at all the sideshows
Have a gamble if you dare!
Watch the little ball that's hopping
Round the circle in roulette,
Should you choose the crown or feather,
Twelve to one against your bet.

Why not try the cardboard horses?
Pick a number or a name,
Watch them run and leap the fences
It's a fantastic game.
There's the gypsy fortune-teller,
Push along and join the queue,
Gazing in the crystal, Lady?
Wonder what's in store for you?

Here you are! Three shots a penny,
Steady does it, one-two-three,
If you hit the bull's eye squarely,
You're a better man than me.
Have a go at pongo? Bingo?
Join the ring and fire ahead,
Watch the board and mark your numbers
Check all yellow, check all red.

★　★　★

Quiet now the hobby-horses,
Time to pack up, time to go.
All the spills and thrills are over,
All the wheels are running low.
Silent now the hurdy-gurdy,
It has played its farewell notes;
Grounded are the dizzy chair-planes
Empty now the swinging boats.

Pale and still the covered wagons,
Ghostly now beneath the moon;
In your ears the haunting rhythm
Of that hurdy-gurdy tune.

Trans-Atlantic Call to
Jim Downey of New York

Across the Atlantic, Jim Downey,
Here's a message from Dublin to you:
We hear that your steaks are so tender
They're the reason why dreams comes true!

But—talking of horses and racing—
The slang is the same, I suppose.
Do they pass the post when they're winning
By a head, or a neck, or a nose?

We 'back' the horses in Dublin
In Galway, Tramore and Kildare.
By your membership card, Jim Downey,
You 'play' them, I see, over there.

We call it the 'racecourse' in Ireland,
In New York it's known as the 'track'.
The name doesn't matter a traneen
When you don't get your money back.

We have bookies with 'stands' on the racecourse,
We've bookies in each city street.
They spring up like mushrooms around us,
Just think of the steaks that they eat!

Do you study the form, and the breeding,
The owner, the trainer, the jock,
And find when the race is all over
That you've backed a three-legged crock?

You place your shirt on your fancy
But he never puts up a spurt,
If there's anything worse than a sucker,
It's a sucker without a shirt!

I'll be over some day, Jim Downey,
Across the Atlantic to you.
Reserve me a shoulder to weep on,
A steak that is tender and true.

Decor

A dash of paint in green or blue,
A bowl of flowers, a book or two:
Such ways and means you might suggest
To rob me of my jackdaw's nest—
The odds and ends that I have stored.
Though I am told I shouldn't hoard,
I've always got the same excuse,
That one day they may prove of use!

You'll find within a dark recess
A broken china shepherdess,
A gramophone, its heyday past,
So silent now and overcast,
A clock that battled through the years
Its tick-tick fallen in arrears,
A locket with a silver chain
(Please don't regard it with disdain!)

A cupid from a wedding cake.
How came he here? It's some mistake!

Two lighters that refuse to light,
Two watches in a sorry plight,
A work-box lined with faded red,
Half-filled with reels of coloured thread.
Buttons of every shape and size,
A card of rusty hooks and eyes,
A broken cup from Grandma's set
(Which gives me cause for much regret!)

I see you smile indulgently;
You wonder how such things can be.
You'd sweep away the entire lot
And make that shelf the brightest spot!
A dash of paint in green or blue,
A bowl of flowers, a book or two,
Such ways and means you might suggest
But *No!* I'll keep my jackdaw's nest!

Parking Space

A river-boat, a pent-house, a chalet by the sea,
An igloo in Alaska, a villa in Capri—
Where would you settle down if you were fancy free?

A mews in Bohemia where highbrows scintillate?
An attic in Montmartre where artists congregate?
Or a skyline apartment in New Jersey State?

A bungalow to purchase? A studio to let?
A one-room basement with a tiny kitchenette?
A villa in suburbia? A cosy maisonette?

What about that haunted house—it's still unoccupied.
Behind the crumbling windows a pair of owls reside
And watch the headless horseman on his midnight ride . . .

You might settle for a cottage down a country lane
Where the cock crows so lustily—lord of his domain—
There you could write your memoirs or make a daisy-chain!

But I am going to Wexford to a stretch of golden sand
Sheltered by the mountains that keep vigil close at hand,
'Tis there I'll park my caravan in no-man's land.

Herself

Next door to us was a pastrycook's
Opposite the 'Horse and Hare'.
Up the street and through the town
You'd sniff those doughnuts, golden brown,
As far as Market Square.

At Easter we had hot-cross buns,
And pancakes every Shrove;
At Christmas piping hot mince-pies
With luscious cakes of every size
Baked in that ancient stove!

If you passed by that pastry shop
You'd see Herself within,
Handing out goodies left and right,
Rosy and plump in her spotless white,
Flour on her dimpled chin . . .

Herself is gone. The shop is now
A noisy snack affair;
Juke boxes moan and groan all day,
Causing annoyance and dismay
Within the 'Horse and Hare'.

Where, oh where is my pastry cook—
She of the dimpled chin?
Somewhere beyond the starry skies
Making angel cakes in Paradise
For all who venture in!

Heirloom

It's a cloth embroidered with tulips
But I cannot guess how old;
I've treasured it since it came to me,
And sometimes I find—in fantasy—
A story in each fold.

Of what did she dream through endless days
As the petals formed and grew;
Her thoughts far off as she bowed her head,
Sorting strands of embroidery thread
In colours clear and true?

Was she youthful, gay and full of dreams,
Or sad through the lonely hours,
Weaving her memories as they came,
Sunlight and shadow, a face, a name,
Among embroidered flowers?

The perfume of lavender is here
As we unwrap the folds,
Stirring up thoughts of a long lost day—
But nothing is left that might betray
The secret that it holds.

Her story is lost. The cloth remains
With its simple old-world grace;
The tulips still live, now she is gone.
I'll cherish it 'til I pass it on
To those who take my place.

Christmas Echoes

I hear the songs of carol singers as their voices ring
    out from a distant street,
The honk of horns, the grinding of brakes, the endless tramp,
    tramp of a thousand feet—

The roar of traffic, the zoom of planes, the rumble of buses,
    the din in the shops,
The chatter of children, the blare of radios, the old-time
    tunes, the latest pops—

The crackle of logs, the swish of balloons, the firing of crackers,
    the postman's knock,
The sing-song voices of souvenir sellers, the whirring of toys,
    the chiming clock—

The sizzle of turkeys, the clatter of dishes, the gentle slam
    of the oven door,
The beat of the drum, the swirl of dresses, the tapping of feet
    on a polished floor—

The laughter, the greetings, the popping of corks, the cheery toast,
    the tinkle of glass,
The peal of bells, the hymns of praise, the murmured blessing,
    the organ's swell, the Midnight Mass.

So Many Things

From Muinterown across the fields we raced,
Stopping for a moment by the hedge to taste
The wild, wet blackberries. So many things—
That bunch of primroses hidden in the lane,
That bearded goat who viewed us with disdain.

Down from the hills the river swept in spate
Across the stepping-stones. Why should I hesitate,
When she was always there to rescue me,
To guide my feet from stone to stone
Until I had the confidence to cross alone?

Through Culliaghbeg we ran, through Thievnamong,
Over the stile we tumbled, breathless, flushed and young.
If we were late for school, she took the blame
And stood in brave defence of me.
Just as she did through all the years 'til yesterday . . .

The rowan trees trembled as the evening came,
The whispering river seemed to speak her name;
I saw again the seven stepping-stones
The wooded cliff, the ivied wall,
The curlew circled low—I heard his lonely call.

Christmas Quest

Tall red candles in each window
Cast their shadowed, flickering light
In a house we well remember
Through the hours of Christmas night.
Children, starry-eyed with wonder,
Watched the drifting flakes of snow;
You and I were there among them
Keeping vigil, long ago.

Is that chair beside the hearthstone
Still reserved for one alone?
Have the books familiar titles
Much the same as we had known?
Over by the corner window
Is that photograph the same?
Perhaps it's blurred with age and faded
In its quaint old-fashioned frame.

Is the little walled-in garden
Fertile as it used to be?
Are the reddest holly berries
Still too high upon the tree?
When the hoar frost grips the meadow
And the morning air is chill,
Does the redbreast call for breakfast
Served upon the window-sill?

Back across the years we travel
As our Christmas dreams take form,
Like lost children home returning
Seeking shelter from the storm.

Growing Up

It seems but yesterday since he was just a toddler
His tear-stained face beseeching—then suddenly a smile!
Long intervals of quiet warned of mischief brewing
Until he curled up in sleep and there was peace awhile.

From cuddly toys of childhood and treasured teddy-bears
To tricycles and engines he passed with youthful zest;
The fairy-tales and comics enthralled him for a time
Until he graduated to cowboys of the West.

Boyish, with inky fingers and war-scarred knobbly knees,
Absorbed in strange mechanics for hours he seemed content.
And football field engrossed him when other interests waned,
Goldfish lasted for a spell, stamp albums came and went.

Soon the muddy shoes, the careless socks, the rumpled hair,
The sudden endless questions, the rough and tumble play
Had vanished—and a youth, his self-reliance growing,
Worked out his own solutions when problems came his way.

And now? Why, now I take advice with meek submission
(How can he make decisions with such apparent ease?).
This is a man's clear thinking mind—and here I wonder
If it were yesterday I patched those broken knees?

Memories

A trim school-hat with a badge I knew
(And holidays start in June)
Bobbed this way and that lightheartedly
Through the crowds one afternoon.
On memory's wings I drifted back
To my school-days, carefree and fleet:
Classroom, library, study-hall,
Laughter of playtime—hush of Retreat.

There were questions I wanted to ask:
"Are the shadowed walks still there?
Do the solemn noonday bells ring out
For the daily Angelus prayer?
Does the sunlight linger on stained-glass panes
Lighting chancel and nave within?
Do the cloisters echo the organ's note
As twilight closes in?"

Other questions I wanted to ask:
"Are those photographs still by the stair?
Do you sometimes smile at our old-fashioned guise
Grouped primly, awkwardly, there?
Have you vanquished Euclid, Irish, French,
Studied Shakespeare line by line?
Or were you involved in schoolgirl pranks—
Had you escapades like mine?"

It bobbed lightheartedly out of sight,
That hat with the badge I knew.
My eager questions remained unasked
Leaving pictures that memory drew.

Gift for a Lady

Shopping for your present lady
Is a very special quest,
And I mean to squander royally
You deserve the very best . . .
Window gazing, so bewildered,
Puzzling out your special line,
I see others bravely facing
Problems just the same as mine!

Here are gloves in lace and crochet,
Sheepskin, fur and softest suede,
Handkerchiefs of purest linen,
Cocktail bags in rich brocade.
On I venture, vacillating,
Treasures lurk on every side
Fevered shoppers all around me
How on earth can I decide?

Fragrant perfumes, gold-tipped bottles,
Handbags difficult to choose,
Purses, wallets, dressing-cases,
Scarves in all their brilliant hues.
Pearls, brooches, jewelled ear-rings,
Chunky bracelets—quite absurd—
Petticoats with foamy laces
Fascinating is the word!

Must not buy you luscious chocolates
Thereby adding to your weight,
You will say I've no discretion
But my dear, it's getting late . . .
Say, those mules are quite enchanting
With their saucy pink rosettes.
Lady, won't you please forgive me—
Would you like some cigarettes?

Midnight Matinée

Strange ghostly sounds disturbed my rest deep in the dead of night;
Though almost paralysed with fear I contemplated flight.
The tongs lurched out on bandy legs, wearing a tall silk hat,
The poker swayed in drunken glee and sprawled across the mat.

A pack of cards played ghostly Bridge—a most fantastic scene,
The Jack of Spades, that surly Knave, shot down his King and Queen.
Instead of ticking, as it should, the clock began to bray,
A tumbler and a tablespoon played tick-tack on my tray!

A blood-red orange bared its teeth, emerging from its peel,
The flowers shook out their gory locks and danced an eight-hand reel;
Grey ghosts came lurking through the dusk and leaned across my bed,
Then icy fingers gripped my hair 'til I was numb with dread.

But when I tried to summon strength to calm my fevered brain,
A face, with bloodshot eyes, appeared outside the window pane,
The wardrobe door flew open wide, a skeleton slipped out,
And as it staggered towards me, I gave a strangled shout . . .

Then as the ghastly gruesome thing nearer and nearer drew,
I heard a casual voice remark: "She's got a touch of flu!"

Gay Deceiver

He checked in there on Monday week,
A man of truly fine physique
With flashing teeth and manly pipe—
He was the big broad-shouldered type—
A veritable sheik!

Tuesday: enchanted by his grin,
The set of his determined chin,
We felt he'd leap a five-barred gate
Or drive a golf ball clean and straight
And land it at the pin!

Wednesday: inclined to criticise
We found more time to analyse,
Beginning to suspect in fact
That all this breezy outdoor act
Was merely a disguise!

Thursday: his smile became a leer,
His molars stacked from ear to ear,
We told each other he was dumb
With nothing but a vacuum
Beneath his thin veneer.

Friday: he proved a dancing fan,
But how could that explain his tan?
He may have bought it down the street,
It certainly looked counterfeit
Exactly as the man!

How wrong indeed was our surmise,
Last Saturday to our surprise,
Playing off a handicap of four
He had a most stupendous score
And won the Captain's prize!

The Shopping Spirit

Through the crowded city pavements,
Heedless now of traffic laws,
Fevered shoppers in a hurry
Little people in a flurry
All agog for Santa Claus.

Would she like exotic perfume?
Fur-lined gloves expressed in suede?
Here are trinkets, quite amusing,
Handbags need some careful choosing,
Emphasis upon the shade.
What a horde of crazy ear-rings
Chunky bracelets—quite absurd;
Purses, wallets, dressing-cases,
Petticoats with foamy laces,
Fascinating is the word!

(Madam? Sure, you're in a hurry
But you mustn't break the queue;
Should I laugh the pain to scorn
As you trample my pet corn
Grind your heel against my shoe?)

Here are rings with gems that sparkle
Brooches too that subtly tone,
Dainty watches—too expensive
And I cannot float a loan!
There's a stole in soft angora,
How those colours harmonise!
But I'm left to cut a caper
While it's wrapped in tissue paper
Carried off before my eyes!

Have you done your shopping early?
Me? I've only just begun.
Shop in comfort? I should hate it
And I'd never feel elated
Missing all the Christmas fun.

The Old Side-Car

Out in the shed there's an old side-car
But its day is long since past.
The corduroy cushions that graced each side,
Tattered and torn, are gaping wide
And the wood is chipping fast.
Gone are the days of the trusty steed,
We've got automobiles instead.
That rush along at a break-neck speed
And nobody pays the slightest heed
To the side-car in the shed.

There was a time—believe it or not—
When it dazzled the village street:
The harness shining, with never a spot,
While Victor went at an easy trot,
Grandpa in the driving seat.
And Grandma would sit, wrapped up in her shawl,
Round her knees the blue plaid rug,
The storm might rage and the rain might fall,
She could afford to smile through it all
She was so cosy and snug!

Though the old side-car is beyond repair
And the wheels will turn no more,
I can see it still in the market square
When Grandpa attended the village fair
In those simple days of yore.
But why do I dream when I see that car
Of the days that used to be?
Grandpa was a man that I much admired
And he was the husband that I acquired—
For Grandmama was me!

Neighbours

Here where the mountains steeply flank the shadowed sea below
Along the narrow mountain road our neighbours come and go.
But should they stop beside our door, from places far or near,
Across our threshold ring the words: "God save and bless all here!"

An old man on his morning stroll with time on hands to spare
Might saunter in to light his pipe and take the fireside chair
To talk of floods and storms that raged in long forgotten days
To ask for news of war and peace, to censure or to praise;
While women coming from the shop exchanging simple views
Will lay their shopping baskets down to share the village news.
And there might come along the path where mountain streams cascade
A shepherd seeking truant sheep that from the flock have strayed.

Grey with the dust of many roads and browned by sun and rain
The wandering gypsies pitch their camp in yonder sheltered lane
Beside his donkey lazily, a youngster ambles by
From low lying bogs returning home with creels of turf piled high
A mower passes with a scythe across his shoulder laid
The meadow dew still damp upon the curve of shining blade
And currachs coming up the bay, each boat a dusky patch
At sundown beach upon the strand to land their silvery catch.

The cliffs beyond the Head grow blurred as twilight hours take flight
And little walled-in meadows sleep beneath the veil of night.
At points along the mountain road the cottage lights appear
We're safely home beside our hearths: "God save and bless all here!"

The Bridal Veil

We find it safely treasured in a nest of tissue paper,
Its secrets wrapped within it, its gallant tale untold;
Only the dreams of yesterday, romances long forgotten,
Only a scent of lavender emerging from each fold.

We ponder on the workmanship, the finely-wrought design,
And find another pattern, a story of the years:
The crowded church, the organ's peal, the heady scent of roses,
The speeches at the wedding feast, the toasting and the cheers.

Had she beauty who first wore it, this veil of Limerick lace,
The grace of it around her as she fluttered up the aisle?
Was it she who cherished it and gently placed within it
Sweet-scented bags of lavender in true old-fashioned style?

Now faded is the story we try to piece together,
And vanished is the setting we endeavour to recast;
But still the spell surrounds it, for now its mellowed beauty
Will lend each bride who wears it the enchantment of the past.

Happy Couples

When I'm fumbling in the kitchen
Wrestling bravely with the pan
Thoughts come back of dear Great-Grandma,
How she catered for her man!
Do you think she'd ring the butcher
Even if she had a phone?
Not at all! She'd go in person
And examine every bone.

All her stocks were neatly labelled
With housewifely pride and care,
Tucked away in airtight bottles
Or in jars of earthenware.
And each label, neatly printed,
With Great-Gran's old-fashioned quill,
Always stood a silent witness
To her culinary skill.

In the fashion of good housewives,
Her plum puddings could be seen
Dangling from the kitchen ceiling
Some days after Halloween!
And when spring was in the meadows,
Sure there is no doubt at all
But she still had last year's pudding
When her cronies came to call.

Pressure cookers, vacuum cleaners
Came too late for poor Great-Gran;
Lots of elbow grease and soap suds
Kept her kitchen spick and span.
And Great-Grandpa was so solid,
Were they happy, he and she?
We're a happy couple also—
My tin-opener and me.

Traffic Jam

Road up—diversion—men at work,
Behind a barricade they lurk!
Danger ahead—drive slowly—STOP!
Keep your eye on the traffic cop . . .
But what is this? A one-way street?
Before you're caught—reverse—retreat!

No Parking? Quick, he's on your track,
Turn her into that cul-de-sac;
Out, out again, there's a traffic jam
With scarcely room to park a pram!
"Hi there, what do you think you're doing?"
(Who's that cheeky chap pursuing?)

Hemmed in, we panic, look out for squalls,
Then suddenly our engine stalls.
St Christopher! The lights turn green,
Oncoming traffic blocks the scene,
Small boys giggle, shoppers stare,
While all together the horns blare . . .

It's over—yes, it's over now
And we survive, I don't know how;
But when we think we've saved our skin
A motor-cycling cop pulls in.
Again we're shaking at the knees:
"Your licence and insurance please!"

He Who Hesitates

Must I cross? And risk my neck?
Look at me, a nervous wreck.
See that man—how he strides,
And that schoolboy—how he slides.
Must be true, in the frost—
"He who hesitates is lost" . . .

Goodness me!

Me? I'm just a looker-on
Cannot cross the Rubicon.
Turn back? Admit defeat?
Take my courage in both feet?
Must get there, weal or woe,
Grit my teeth and here I go . . .

Look at me!

Half-way there. Nearly over.
Nonchalant. Then I hover.
There's a car, let it pass,
One-step, two-step, road like glass.
Screech of brakes, crown around
Dear old lady on the ground . . .

Guess it's me!

The Animal Express

Standing in the railway station,
Passengers all animation
Full of fun and jubilation,
Was the Animal Express.
What a sight, and how amazing!
Saw a tigress round her gazing
Haughtily her lorgnette raising
In an effort to impress.

An elephant was baby-sitting
And a nanny-goat was knitting,
Occupations unbefitting
On the Animal Express.
In a bath-tub frogs were croaking,
Two giraffes were busy stoking,
Polar bears were idly smoking,
Somewhat lacking in finesse!

Saw a fox on chicken thriving
And a pair of seals skin-diving,
While a chimpanzee was driving
Wearing regulation dress.
At a whist drive, sheep were bleating,
Lots of rabbits were competing,
Sad to see the walrus cheating
In the Animal Express.

Saw a lioness old and hoary
Telling cubs a bed-time story,
How she in her youthful glory
Ruled the jungle with success.
In the better class division
Pussy waiters in collision,
Greyhounds watching television
Well-bred horses playing chess.

Kerry Blue, the station master,
Had his nose in sticking plaster.
Doggy rows will cause disaster
Squabbles ending in distress.
Loudly then the whistle sounded,
All aboard, late comers bounded,
With a flourish off it pounded
That old Animal Express.

Poor Kate

They're huddled together beside your cot:
Laura, who's always sedate,
Then cute little picanniny Sue
Of the curly hair and the dusky hue,
And one-eyed scallywag Kate!
Your playmates view them with critical eyes:
Laura, who looks like a queen,
Susan, whom children love to hug,
But Kate just gets an indifferent shrug
In her tattered frock of green.

For Laura has silvery buckled shoes
And a bracelet of shining stones,
Susan has petticoats trimmed with lace
But scallywag Kate has a battered face
And several broken bones.
One stormy night when the thunder crashed
And we watched the lightning dart,
Laura and Susan were left to their fate
While you ran to rescue scallywag Kate
And held her close to your heart . . .
But afterwards when the storm had passed
You explained to Laura and Sue:
"Kate was afraid when the lightning came,
So I held her tight, 'cause she's old and lame
And she cannot run like you!"

Her Master's Voice

I hear your voice on the intercom
So I suffer a moment's tension.
You seem to be calm, there's no urgency yet,
But I'll be right there should you fumble or fret
Or call for immediate attention!

But soon I detect a louder note,
You're cross, my dear man, and you show it!
You must realise it's the end of the day—
Though I'd work overtime without any pay
For you, my dear chap, and you know it!

But now I'm lost in a world of dreams
(Forgetting about the extension!)
All the neighbours are talking of our affair
Let them chatter and gossip—I just don't care,
For I love you beyond redemption.

Comes a warning note from the intercom
Has something occurred to distress you?
This time you have made a more urgent demand
So I rush to your side with bottle in hand:
It's your feeding time—and God bless you!

Lost Leader

Your mighty task
Was yet a friendly task,
Discarding ancient precepts now outgrown;
Within the clutter of a tangled world
You strove to build an edifice of stone.

Your gifted hands
Were steady, guiding hands,
That gripped the rudder when the storm rode high
And, steering darkly towards the shore of peace,
You glimpsed the sunlight in tomorrow's sky.

Your simple words
Yet dedicated words
Gave sympathetic counsel or command;
With hope in you, and firm belief in you,
Men looked into the future that you planned.

Your far-seeing eyes
Were yet a dreamer's eyes
That saw the distant clouds suffused with light;
The darkness came—a moment's puzzlement
Before all things were blotted from your sight.

Golden Jubilee

Soft footsteps echo through the cloistered halls
Where stained-glass panes reflect the twilight's glow;
The organ's note swells out in hymns of praise
And in the choir veiled heads are bowed low.

Like Ave Marias in the Rosary
Those fifty golden years have flown
Through five decades—each bead a golden year:
In lifetime's crown, each year a precious stone.

Here in the tutored wisdom of the years,
The knowledge never gleaned from printed page;
Here, counsel might be given which could reach
Beyond the scope of savant or of sage.

Though here was joy and happiness complete
Sadness there must have been, and hidden tears—
But both were interwoven in a prayer
Pleading its way through fifty golden years.

Footprints

Someday I'll rest my head beside
the purple heather,
And slowly I'll retrace the footprints
Time has made;
Some will be clear and well-defined,
Some fresh as yesterday,
Some hesitant, uncertain, as of a
child who strayed.

Someday I'll take my rest beside
the purple heather,
And watch the distant peaks outlined
against the sky;
Before the darkness falls, I'll hear
the voice of childhood,
Within the lonely valley
Where no one passes by.